Science and Technology

Green Technology

John Coad

www.raintreepublishers.co.uk
Visit our website to find out more information about Raintree books.

To order:
☏ Phone 0845 6044371
🖷 Fax +44 (0) 1865 312263
✉ Email myorders@raintreepublishers.co.uk

Customers from outside the UK please telephone +44 1865 312262

Raintree is an imprint of Capstone Global Library Limited, a company incorporated in England and Wales having its registered office at 7 Pilgrim Street, London, EC4V 6LB – Registered company number: 6695582

Text © Capstone Global Library Limited 2012
First published in hardback in 2012
Papernack edition first published in 2013
The moral rights of the proprietor have been asserted.

Edited by Andrew Farrow, Adam Miller, and Diyan Leake
Designed by Victoria Allen
Original illustrations © Capstone Global Library Ltd 2011
Illustrated by Oxford Designers & Illustrators
Picture research by Elizabeth Alexander
Originated by Capstone Global Library Ltd
Printed and bound in China by CTPS

ISBN 978 1 406 22839 7 (hardback)
15 14 13 12 11
10 9 8 7 6 5 4 3 2 1

ISBN 978 1 406 22849 6 (paperback)
16 15 14 13 12
10 9 8 7 6 5 4 3 2 1

British Library Cataloguing in Publication Data
Coad, John.
  Science and technology: green technology. -- (Sci-hi)
  600-dc22
A full catalogue record for this book is available from the British Library.

Acknowledgements
The author and publishers are grateful to the following for permission to reproduce copyright material: Alamy pp. **30** (© Borderlands), **43** (© Andia); Corbis pp. **6** (© Luke Macgregor/Reuters), **7** (© Reuters), **16** (© Zhai Dong Feng / Redlink), **20** (© Jan Woitas/dpa), **21** (© Transtock), **38** (© Ben Sklar/Reuters); Getty Images pp. **13** (AFP), **15**, **23** (Bloomberg), **37** (John Lamb/Stone); PA Photos p. **25** (AP Photo/Efrem Lukatsky); Photolibrary pp. **8** (Tony Waltham), **12** (Daniel Schoenen/imagebroker.net), **32** (Ian West/OSF); Science Photo Library p. **41** (Lawrence Berkeley National Laboratory); © Seawater Greenhouse Ltd p. **31**; Shutterstock **contents page** top (© Kheng Guan Toh), **contents page** bottom (© Tyler Boyes)pp. **4** (© Dmitriy Kuzmichev), **9** (© VLADJ55), **10** (© Wiktor Bubniak), **14** (© Zacarias Pereira da Mata), **18** (© Kheng Guan Toh), **19** (© charles taylor), **24** (© mirounga), **28** (© Matthew Cole), **29** (© Feng Yu), **34** (© Fred Leonero), **35** (© c.), **36** (© Denis Babenko), **40** (© Tyler Boyes), **all background and design features**; University of York p. **39**.

Main cover photograph of PlanetSolar, the world's largest solar powered boat, reproduced with permission of Getty (Jochen Eckel/Bloomberg); inset cover photograph of colourful LEDs reproduced with permission of shutterstock (© demarcomedia).

The publisher would like to thank literary consultant Nancy Harris and content consultant Suzy Gazlay for their assistance in the preparation of this book.

Every effort has been made to contact copyright holders of material reproduced in this book. Any omissions will be rectified in subsequent printings if notice is given to the publisher.

Disclaimer
All the Internet addresses (URLs) given in this book were valid at the time of going to press. However, due to the dynamic nature of the Internet, some addresses may have changed, or sites may have changed or ceased to exist since publication. While the author and publisher regret any inconvenience this may cause readers, no responsibility for any such changes can be accepted by either the author or the publisher.

Contents

What is biofuel? Turn to page 18 to find out!

What is a nanotube? Read page 40 to find out!

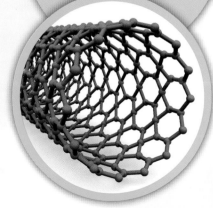

Some words are shown in bold, **like this**. These words are explained in the glossary. You will find important information and definitions underlined, <u>like this</u>.

TIME FOR A CHANGE

Many things that we use in our everyday lives are made from Earth's **natural resources**. Natural resources are things that people can use that come from nature. However, if we continue to use up these resources they will one day run out. Humans cannot keep living in this way. It is not **sustainable**. This means that it cannot go on for ever.

We obtain metals from huge mines like this. What will happen when the metal has all been used up?

Thinking about the future

What will happen if we don't think about the future?

- If we keep using up things that nature provides for us, there will be none left in the future.

- If we keep using up **fossil fuels**, like oil and coal, they will run out.

- What will happen to your grandchildren if our sources of **energy** (fuel for heat and light, and to power vehicles) and natural resources have all run out?

If the human race is going to survive, we have to do things differently.

Go green

Green is the colour of healthy plants. It is the colour of nature. "Green" is also used to describe anything that does not harm the **environment**. If technology is green, it does not pollute or waste precious resources.

Throw it away

All the time, we use something and then throw it away. What we need to learn is that there is no such place as "away". Anything we throw away stays on Earth and damages our environment. Green technology aims to reduce the amount that we throw away.

RUNNING OUT OF RESOURCES

Copper is used in our electrical wiring. What will we do when there is no more copper to dig up? Already the cost of copper has gone up because it is harder to find and more and more countries want it.

FANTASTIC PLASTIC

Plastic is made from oil that will one day run out. Plastic is bad in two ways: it uses natural resources and it makes waste. Green technology is beginning to change things by making plastics from plants. As long as we can grow the plants, we can get the plastic. Also, plastic made from plants will rot away in time. <u>Green technology can give us a sustainable way of using plastic.</u>

Green technology looks at ways of making things from materials that will not run out. We must get more energy from sources that will always be available, such as the Sun and wind. Above all, we must change our attitude to waste.

Green technology in action

Green technology looks at the whole life of an object – where it comes from, how it is used, and what happens to it when it is no longer wanted.

Green technology is changing the way we do things. From the way we build houses to the way we **generate** (create) electricity – things are changing. From the way we produce **chemicals** (substances that can be changed into other substances by changing their structure) to the way we travel – green technology is having an impact.

RECYCLING

Recycling is better than throwing things away but is not always the best answer. Collecting and processing old bottles, cans, or newspapers uses lots of energy. It is energy we cannot afford to use. <u>Green technology designs objects so that not much waste is produced</u>. It is not the same as recycling.

BRIGHT IDEA: SAVE MONEY

Many big companies have realized that green technology is good for them. It can reduce their energy bills and save money on the disposing (throwing away) of waste. It is also good publicity – people like to hear of environmentally friendly companies.

Green factory

The Ford Motor Company's factory near Detroit, USA was redeveloped to be green. Inside there are systems to save energy and reduce **pollution**. Outside, the roof is covered with a plant that survives with little water. This covering doubles the life of the roof. It absorbs rainwater – reducing the chances of flooding – and helps prevent heat loss. This all saves the company money. This project has inspired many other companies to go green.

The plant growing on the roof of the Ford factory is called sedum.

GREEN ENERGY

For many years most of our energy has come from burning fossil fuels. These include gas, oil, and coal. We use oil to give us petrol and diesel for our vehicles. We also burn oil, coal, and gas in **power stations** (factories where electricity is produced).

Fossil fuel problems

There are two main problems linked to fossil fuels. Firstly, these natural resources are **non-renewable**. This means they will eventually run out.

A second problem with using fossil fuels is that when we burn them they create carbon dioxide gas. There is more and more carbon dioxide in the air. Most scientists believe this is causing our planet to warm up.

Here, a number of oil wells make up a large oil field. Many countries around the world produce oil from the ground but oil is starting to run out. Once used up, we cannot get more oil. It is non-renewable.

Renewable energy

Other sources of energy will not run out. As long as the Sun shines we can have **solar** power. As long as the wind blows we can have wind power and wave power. These energy sources are **renewable**. Green technology is used to improve how we gain energy from renewable sources.

You can see the smoke coming from this coal-burning power station but you cannot see the carbon dioxide. It is a colourless gas which is produced whenever we burn fossil fuels.

CARBON FOOTPRINT

Energy is needed for everything we do. Energy has been used to create every human-made object we use. If that energy came from burning fossil fuels, then carbon dioxide was pumped into the air. <u>The amount of carbon dioxide released into the air to produce the energy one person uses is called their **carbon footprint**</u>. Green technology aims to reduce everyone's carbon footprints by saving energy and by making it from renewable sources.

9

Wind power

Wind power has been used for hundreds of years to grind corn or pump water. Taking energy from the wind is easier now thanks to green technology. The blades of a windmill drive a **turbine** (machine) which generates (creates) electricity. Turbines can be small, making enough power for just one home. Or they can be large, providing electricity for factories and cities.

Wind farms

When many wind turbines are built together, we call it a wind farm. Australia's biggest wind farm is now being built in the state of New South Wales. With 400 to 500 turbines, the wind farm will create 4.5 per cent of the whole of New South Wales's energy needs. It will supply electricity to over 400,000 homes.

Modern wind turbines are an efficient way of harnessing the power of the wind.

Turbine technology

A wind turbine works the opposite way to a fan. Instead of using electricity to make wind, like a fan, wind turbines use wind to make electricity. Wind turns the blades which then drive a generator (see the picture below). The generator then creates the electricity.

This picture shows the parts of a wind turbine.

ENVIRONMENTAL IMPACT

Wind farms have to be built in the windiest places. These are often on the coast or up on hills. Many people feel this ruins the beauty of natural scenery. Wind turbines are also noisy and can harm birds. More wind farms are now being built in the sea. This is more expensive but it doesn't use up valuable land. Other people who dislike wind farms point out that they cannot produce electricity when there is no wind. As a result, we still need other power stations.

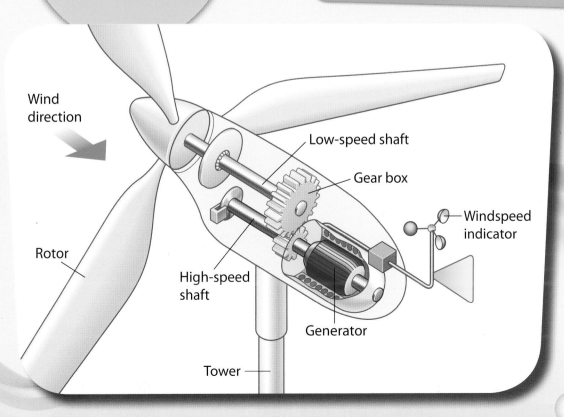

Wind direction

Low-speed shaft

Gear box

Windspeed indicator

Rotor

High-speed shaft

Generator

Tower

FREE ENERGY FROM THE SUN

Solar power has been used for over 100 years to heat water. <u>More recently, scientists have found that some materials absorb (take in) sunlight and produce electricity</u>. This is called the **photovoltaic** effect. This effect was originally seen as a novelty. Then it was used for devices such as light **sensors** in cameras. But the process was not good enough to produce cheap electricity.

Photovoltaic power became more efficient as technology improved. Today, about 12 per cent of the solar energy that beams on to solar panels turns into electricity. This is four times better than even a few years ago. Solar panels are expensive to put in buildings but they will save money over many years.

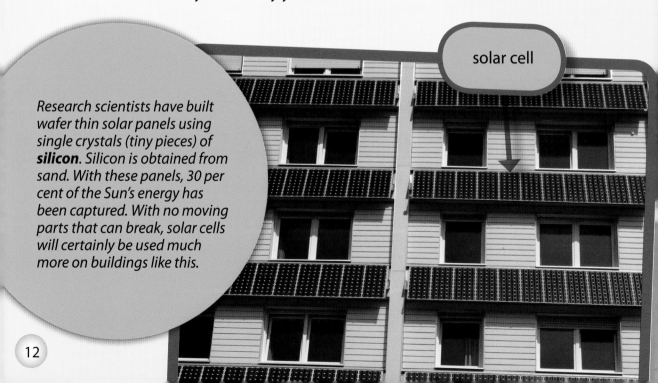

solar cell

*Research scientists have built wafer thin solar panels using single crystals (tiny pieces) of **silicon**. Silicon is obtained from sand. With these panels, 30 per cent of the Sun's energy has been captured. With no moving parts that can break, solar cells will certainly be used much more on buildings like this.*

BRIGHT IDEA: FLY BY NIGHT!

In July 2010 a Swiss aircraft pilot made history. He became the first person to fly a solar powered plane all night long! Called Solar Impulse, the aircraft weighed as much as a small car but its wingspan (the distance from the tip of one wing to the other) was 63 metres (207 feet). This is as wide as a large airliner.

On the wings were 12,000 solar cells. These produced electricity to drive motors. The electricity was also used to charge batteries. At night, the plane could keep flying with power from its batteries. By flying non-stop for 26 hours, it was proved that solar power could work through a whole day.

The next challenge for Solar Impulse is to fly around the world. It has shown it can stay in the air for a long time. This flight has proved that renewable energy can achieve what was thought to be impossible.

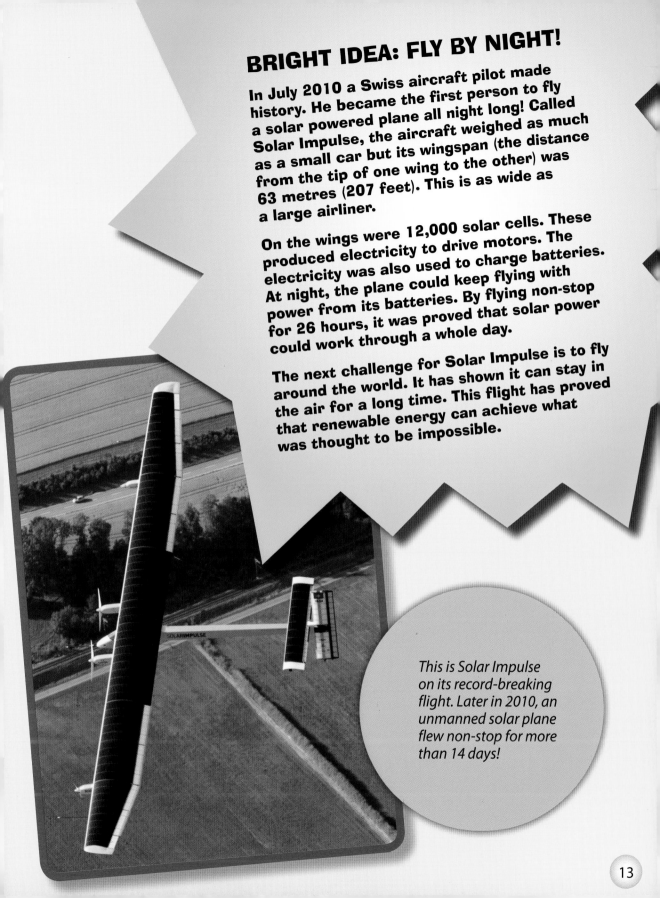

This is Solar Impulse on its record-breaking flight. Later in 2010, an unmanned solar plane flew non-stop for more than 14 days!

ENERGY IN THE OCEANS

Have you ever stood by the sea during a storm? You'll be amazed by the power of the waves – they have so much energy. Scientists have been trying to discover how to capture that energy and turn it into electricity.

One interesting technology is the Pelamis – named after a species of sea snake. The Pelamis is made from connected sections that can bend as waves pass. This bending is used to generate electricity.

Wave energy is a powerful resource.

Go with the flow – energy from tides

Another source of energy that will never run out is the tide. Again, the challenge for engineers is how to turn tidal energy into a form that we can use. One idea is to build barriers across the mouths of large rivers. Water would be allowed through gates as the tide rises and falls, and this would drive generators. Many people do not like this idea as it would change the environment in the river mouth. Animals and plants that live there now may not be able to survive.

SeaGen was built in 2008. The plan is for it to power 1,000 homes.

THE "UNDERWATER WINDMILL"

A simple solution to trying to use the sea's energy has been developed and built in Ireland. Called SeaGen, it is like an underwater windmill. Blades of a turbine are driven by the tidal water flowing in and out. The turbine then generates electricity.

Water

Like the wind, water has been used to create power for hundreds of years. Streams of water were channelled to flow over a water wheel. The wheel would operate machinery. As technology developed, dams were built to hold back water. The water was then allowed to flow through gates and turn turbines, generating electricity. This is called **hydroelectricity**. <u>Hydroelectric power supplies about 20 per cent of the world's electricity</u>.

The Three Gorges Dam

The Three Gorges Dam in China is the world's largest dam. It has been built to generate hydroelectric power and it produces huge amounts of electricity. It also helps to control the flooding that happens on the Yangtze River. However, when it was built, 1.4 million people had to be moved from their homes. Their land was flooded by the huge lake behind the dam.

ENVIRONMENTAL IMPACT

Dams have a huge impact on the environment by flooding land that becomes a reservoir (lake that stores water). The flow of water down a river is also changed and this can affect plants and animals that live along it. Scientists also worry that the huge amount of water behind a dam could cause earthquakes. Landslides and thousands of cracks in the ground suggest this might already be happening around the Three Gorges Dam.

Huge pylons carry the cables that distribute electricity generated from the world's biggest dam.

RUN OF RIVER

In most countries the places that are suitable for building a dam and creating a lake have all been used. In the future it is likely that run-of-river schemes will be used. Run-of-river schemes simply divert (change the path of) some of the water from a river along a pipe. The pipe might be buried under ground. This is done where the river is steepest so water flows fastest. At the end of the pipe, the flowing water turns a turbine and generates electricity. All the water is eventually returned to the river. <u>Run-of-river schemes cause less damage to the environment because no dam is built and the land is not flooded.</u>

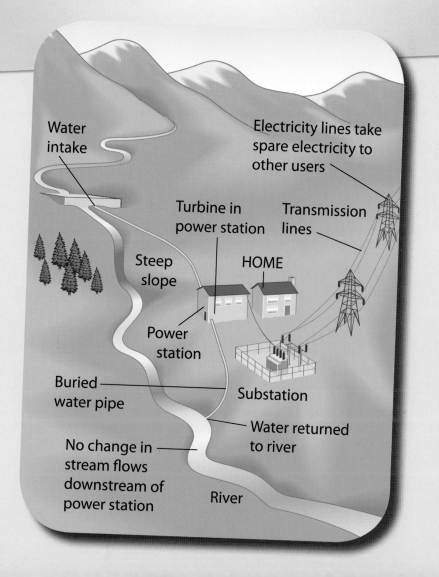

Water intake

Electricity lines take spare electricity to other users

Turbine in power station

Transmission lines

Steep slope

HOME

Power station

Buried water pipe

Substation

Water returned to river

No change in stream flows downstream of power station

River

GROW YOUR OWN FUEL

Technology has found several ways of using living things to produce fuels. These are known as **biofuels** and are renewable. For example:

• Sugar can be turned into alcohol and used in car engines

• Oil from a wide range of plants, such as the oil palm tree, can be turned into diesel fuel. This fuel, called **biodiesel**, can be used for vehicles.

The small palm oil plants in the foreground grow into larger trees, seen further away. Oil is obtained from their seeds.

ALGAE TO DIESEL

The tiny plant-like growing things that make pond water look green are called **algae**. We consider them a nuisance when they cover a lake. A lot of research is being done on producing fuel from algae. Algae grow almost anywhere, have a high energy content, and grow quickly. There are lots of problems to overcome before we can run our cars on fuel from algae. However, many people think algae could produce fuels in the future.

FOREST AND FOOD

In Borneo huge areas of rainforest have been cleared to grow oil palm trees to produce biodiesel. As a result, the habitat (place where something lives) of the orangutan has been destroyed. In other parts of the world, there have been food shortages because land was used to grow biofuels rather than food.

Biofuels are not really green if growing them threatens animals and plants with extinction.

Research goes on

A huge amount of research work is being carried out all around the world to improve the technology of renewable energy. Some sources of energy that we now think are too expensive will become useful in the future. Some of the difficulties in capturing solar, wave, and tidal energy will be solved. You can be certain that the green technology of renewable energy will develop in years to come.

GREEN TRANSPORT

Burning fuel in a car engine makes carbon dioxide gas. This comes out of the exhaust pipe. Making car engines that use less fuel saves oil and money. It also reduces the carbon dioxide given off. Manufacturers try to make cars which do more miles per litre of petrol.

The body of a Formula 1 racing car is made from plastic strengthened with carbon fibre. This gives a very light but very strong structure. It is also very expensive. The technology is not used in ordinary cars.

Saving fuel

Here are some ways to save fuel in a vehicle:

• *Make sure tyres are at the right pressure.* This reduces friction with the ground.

• *Keep to speed limits.* Driving at 85 miles per hour (mph) on a motorway uses 20 per cent more fuel than driving at 70 mph.

• *Reduce weight and air resistance* by removing unnecessary luggage and unused roof racks.

• *Cruise at a steady speed* in the highest possible gear.

• *Try to do without air conditioning.* It increases fuel consumption by 10 per cent.

• *Try to avoid queues.* Every minute spent still in a queue uses petrol unnecessarily.

Only about 15 per cent of the energy from fuel is actually used to move a car. Over 60 per cent is wasted as heat. Some is lost as the engine sits idle and even more is wasted in the linkage between the engine and the drive wheels.

SMARTER CARS

Some cars can adjust as conditions change. They can:

• *have greater power.* A system called turbocharging uses exhaust gases to drive a fan which pushes more air and fuel into the engine.

• *adjust their engine use.* Some cars with large engines of 6 or 8 cylinders now "switch off" cylinders when they are not needed.

• *avoid crashes.* Radar systems around the car make it impossible to crash the car.

The Hummer H2 is sold in the United States. It does only about 12 miles per gallon (5 kilometres per litre). Contrast this with a Fiat Grande Punto which can do about 60 miles per gallon (25 kilometres per litre).

Hybrid cars

A **hybrid** vehicle is one which combines two forms of power. Most hybrid cars combine a petrol engine with an electric motor.

A hybrid car has a petrol engine just like most cars. However, it is smaller, with advanced technology to make it efficient. It also has an electric motor which is powered by batteries. The motor can act as a generator as well. When the car slows down, the generator kicks in and produces electricity to charge the batteries.

The small petrol engine can keep the car moving at a good speed along a flat motorway. However, when the car needs to accelerate (speed up) or go uphill, the electric motor starts up to provide extra thrust (force to make it move). When the car slows down, instead of wasting energy as heat in the brakes, the generator turns it into electricity. Hybrid cars have been very expensive but as their price drops, more people are buying them.

This diagram shows how a hybrid car works.

How hybrid cars use energy

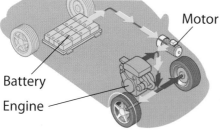
Motor
Battery
Engine

1. Engine receives help from electric motor when accelerating. This means a smaller engine can be used.

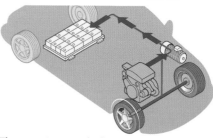

2. The engine and electric motor turn energy from petrol to energy stored in batteries. This can be used when needed.

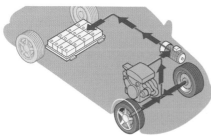

3. Using the brakes drives the electric motor, storing the energy in the battery.

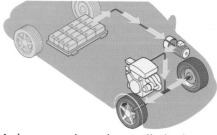

4. At low speed or when still, the battery provides all the car's energy needs.

ELECTRIC CARS

Cars that run on a battery sounds like a good idea. However, electric vehicles have never been very successful. Batteries are large and heavy and have to be charged regularly. The vehicles have been slow. Now advanced technology has produced lighter, smaller batteries and better motors. Electric cars can now go faster and further.

HOW GREEN IS IT?

Electric cars do not give off any gases and seem to cause no pollution. But where does the electricity come from to charge the batteries? If it is made in power stations which burn fossil fuels, the pollution is still created. So we need to produce electricity in a sustainable way. Perhaps in time cars will have solar panels and use them to charge batteries, just like the aeroplane on page 13.

This new design of electric car is on sale in Japan and the United States.

Green aircraft

An aircraft uses lots of fuel and produces huge amounts of carbon dioxide and other **greenhouse gases**. Aircraft also cause noise pollution. Now aircraft manufacturers are aiming to build aeroplanes that are quieter, use less fuel, and produce less harmful **emissions**. Emissions are substances that are released into the air. In Europe a project called "Clean Sky" has manufacturers working together to produce environmentally friendly aircraft.

The Dreamliner

The world's biggest aeroplane maker – Boeing in the United States – has developed the Dreamliner. This can carry up to 300 passengers and is the most fuel-efficient aircraft the company has ever built. The body is built from plastic strengthened with carbon fibre. This makes the aeroplane lighter so it uses less fuel. It produces 20 per cent less carbon dioxide than the aeroplanes it replaces.

Some people say that the way the Dreamliner saves fuel will make air travel cheaper. More people will fly and there will be no environmental benefits.

New types of engine

Another approach is to change the type of jet engine. Open **rotor** engines have blades outside the engine itself. These provide more thrust (force to make the plane move), which makes the engine more fuel efficient. Although they are not as powerful as normal jets, it is likely that the savings on fuel will persuade airlines to use them. One problem to overcome is that these engines are even noisier than normal jets.

Airlines worry that passengers might not like the open rotor engines. They look like old-fashioned propellers.

FLYING ON FAT

Even the US military is going green! An FA18 fighter jet has been using a mixture of normal fuel and oil obtained from a plant. Pilots couldn't tell the difference between normal fuel and the new mixture. In another project, oil has been made from animal fat to power planes.

GREEN BUILDINGS

In countries such as the United Kingdom and the United States, buildings use nearly half the energy produced. Lots of this energy is wasted as heat. Around one-third of the heat loss from a house happens through the walls. Simple technologies that prevent this are easy to use. The starting point is good **insulation**.

Start simply

Insulators stop heat passing through them. They will keep a house warm in winter and cool in summer. Here are some examples.

- Fill cavities (gaps) between two layers of brick with insulating material

- Fit double glazed windows

- Add an insulating layer either on the inside or outside of a house if you have solid walls

- Add insulation underneath floor boards

- Insulate the loft

- Fill gaps to prevent draughts

- Insulate hot water tank and pipes

In Germany, a style of building has become known as a "passive house". The insulation is so good that it does not need a heating system. Thousands of homes have now been built to this standard. In Sweden, there is a new museum open to the public that is a passive house. It uses heat from the equipment inside and from the bodies that visit it to keep it warm.

New ways of keeping warm

In some sustainable buildings, a heat pump takes heat from the ground and uses it in the underfloor heating. Fan coil units have water pumped through them to warm or cool a room.

To build an environmentally friendly, sustainable house, it is important to plan carefully first. Designers or architects will try to include many of the ideas shown here.

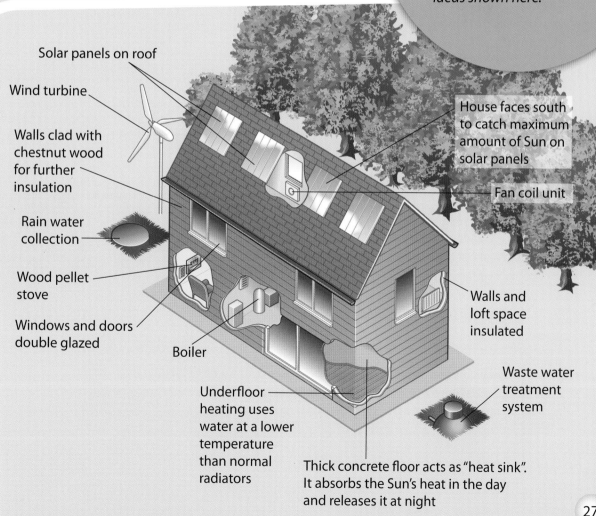

Solar panels on roof

Wind turbine

Walls clad with chestnut wood for further insulation

Rain water collection

Wood pellet stove

Windows and doors double glazed

Boiler

House faces south to catch maximum amount of Sun on solar panels

Fan coil unit

Walls and loft space insulated

Waste water treatment system

Underfloor heating uses water at a lower temperature than normal radiators

Thick concrete floor acts as "heat sink". It absorbs the Sun's heat in the day and releases it at night

A lot of energy is wasted in buildings such as these office blocks in Singapore.

Light up

Go into any big city at night and you'll see office blocks with their lights blazing brightly. Often workers stay late in the evening. There is often no fixed time for offices to close and lights to be turned out. Simple technology can solve the problem. Many companies have installed movement sensors. As long as people are moving around, the lights stay on. Once movement stops, the lights are automatically turned off.

Better bulbs

Electric light bulbs were first made with thin wires that glow brightly when an electric current flows through them. They glow because the wire gets very hot. In fact, 90 per cent of electrical energy is turned into heat energy and wasted. **Fluorescent** lights use 75 per cent less energy and create only one-quarter of the heat. A 23-watt fluorescent tube gives as much light as a 100-watt traditional bulb.

Nothing's perfect

The technology of fluorescent tubes has developed so that we now have very compact bulbs. However, these bulbs contain small amounts of mercury. Mercury is a poisonous chemical. For this reason, fluorescent bulbs should be recycled, not thrown away.

Some people do not like the new fluorescent bulbs. This is because the bulbs emit (give off) more blue wavelengths of light that don't feel so cosy to sit in. Some people are more comfortable with the old bulbs that give off light with more red in it.

THE FUTURE?

In the 1960s, electronic items called light-emitting diodes (LEDs) were first introduced. They shone red and were used as warning lamps or on–off lamps on many devices. Technology has improved and now they are suitable for home lighting. There are still problems to overcome. One LED still cannot produce as much light as a normal bulb and generally they are not as efficient as a fluorescent tube. However, in 2010 one manufacturer claimed to have made a super-efficient LED. Expect to see these low-energy, non-toxic (not harmful) devices used more in the future.

From long tubes to new coiled designs, fluorescent bulbs have changed a lot. Expect them to improve even further in the future.

RECYCLING WATER

When we wash dishes, do our laundry, or have a shower the waste is known as "greywater". Usually this is run off down drains to join toilet waste on the way to the sewers. However, greywater can be used for watering plants and flushing toilets. It must be treated first because it might contain harmful **bacteria** (tiny living things which can cause disease). Greywater can be stored in a tank and treated to kill the bacteria.

Harvesting rain

Modern **eco-houses** (environmentally friendly houses) collect rainwater for use in washing machines and for flushing toilets. This is known as rainwater harvesting. This can change some people's lives. In parts of Africa people have to walk several kilometres each day to collect clean water from a well. Giving them the equipment to collect rainwater can save them the exhausting walk and provide enough water for crops.

Simple green technology can easily improve the lives of many people.

Our most precious resource

As climates around the world change, it is predicted that water shortages will increase. Water could become our most precious resource. <u>While there is plenty of water on Earth, nearly 97 per cent of it is in the oceans and is not fit for us to use.</u> Treating seawater to remove the salt requires energy and is expensive. However, a new process has been developed that uses solar energy. Salt water is heated to make steam (a gas). When this is then cooled it becomes pure water (a liquid). This is called solar distillation.

THE THEATRE OF WATER

Can solar distillation be scaled up and used in other places? One architect certainly thinks so. He has designed a theatre for Spain's Canary Islands which will produce clean water from seawater. Called Teatro del Agua ("Theatre of Water"), the building will act as a theatre for performing arts and produce fresh water. Using energy from the sea, sun, and wind, salty water will be evaporated (turned into a gas) then condensed (liquified) back using deep seawater to cool the steam.

This is an artist's impression of what the Teatro del Agua will look like.

GREEN MATERIALS

Green technology looks at the whole lifespan of materials – where they came from and where they will end up. In building eco-houses, recycled materials are often used. Otherwise, materials are chosen that have not used large amounts of energy in their manufacture or transport.

Recycled materials

Some examples of recycled materials are:

• *Building blocks made by compressing ashes*. When waste materials are burnt in incinerators (furnaces) ashes are left behind.

• *Wood obtained locally from managed forests*. It is fine to use wood as long as trees are replanted.

• *Lambswool for insulation of walls and loft spaces*. This uses a tiny amount of energy compared with the making of other insulation.

Using wood from these chestnut trees can be a sustainable way of providing insulation for houses.

Smart buildings

Smart materials change in a particular way when weather conditions change. For example they might change when heated, or when they get wet. Architects believe that smart materials could change the way buildings are designed.

Just suppose a building became whiter when the Sun shone. More heat and light would be reflected away. On a dull day the building would be darker to absorb more solar energy. These are great ideas but are very expensive to include in a building. This kind of house would save money eventually but costs a lot to set up.

Smart glass

Buildings with large windows can become too hot in the summer and difficult to keep warm in the winter. Smart glass can change all that! With the touch of a button an operator can change the glass from transparent (allows all light to pass through) to translucent (allows some light to pass through). This helps with temperature control, saving heating and air conditioning costs.

One designer has developed curtain-like hangings that will capture solar energy. Just imagine producing your electricity from photovoltaic curtains! At present the material is too expensive but the idea and the technology are certain to be developed.

GREEN CHOICES

Some materials that are not green are still used. An example is concrete. Whenever concrete is made, carbon dioxide is released. But a thick floor of concrete is useful in a house as it absorbs heat in the day and releases it at night. As with many environmental issues, there is no simple answer. We have to weigh up advantages and disadvantages.

COPYING NATURE

Steel, concrete, and glass are produced at high temperatures and so consume a lot of energy. In nature, strong materials – such as animal shells – are made using little energy. Scientists are trying to copy nature by finding new, lighter, low-energy materials that are strong enough for buildings.

GREEN CHEMISTRY

From plastics to cosmetics, electronic components to paints, medicines to fertilizers we use huge amounts of chemicals. The chemical industry has always used up raw materials (natural resources such as oil and minerals from the ground), as well as lots of energy. The processes to make chemicals often produce waste – some of it toxic. Some of the chemical products are thrown away.

Going green

Green chemistry aims to change the way we make chemicals. Wherever possible, materials are obtained from renewable sources. Processes are changed so waste is not produced. What happens when the product is no longer required is also considered. Can the chemical be reused or recycled? Is it **biodegradable** (does it break down naturally)?

Could crops like this provide the plastics of the future? If so, will we still be able to grow enough food?

Lead-free solder

This picture shows the type of circuit (track) that we find in most electrical devices. Parts of the circuit have been joined together by shiny metal. The metal is called solder. It melts easily so is used to make the connections. Lead is a metal that is easy to melt and so it is used in solder. However, it is poisonous. It has also been used in batteries and paints. Green chemistry has found other materials instead of lead to give us safer soldering materials, batteries, and paints.

New plastics

Plastics made from plants, such as corn or potatoes, are a green chemistry success story. Already we can buy plastic knives and forks made from potato starch. We can also buy biodegradable packaging made from corn. Corn rots away naturally, leaving no waste.

Safer packaging

Expanded polystyrene is a plastic material used as packaging. In the past, gases called chlorofluorocarbons (CFCs) were blown through the polystyrene to bubble it up. CFCs are harmful to the environment. Now green chemistry has shown that waste carbon dioxide can be used instead. An even better solution is not to use expanded polystyrene and replace it with plastics from plants.

Making medicines

Ibuprofen is a painkiller that many people use. To make it, hazardous chemicals are used and a lot of waste is produced. A new green chemistry method now reduces waste, prevents pollution, and saves energy.

Copying nature

Living things make very complicated chemicals from natural materials without making harmful waste. Often this can be done because living things use special chemicals called **enzymes**. Using living things – or substances taken from them – to make products we want is called **biotechnology**.

Fermentation

A simple example of biotechnology is the making of alcohol. We can make alcohol from oil but it uses lots of energy (as well as the oil) and some harmful chemicals. Nature does it much better through **fermentation**. A simple fungus (plant-like growing thing) called yeast contains enzymes that can turn sugar into alcohol. The only waste is carbon dioxide. Fermentation is also used to make medicines such as antibiotics, food flavouring, and a vitamin.

Here beer is brewed in large tanks. This is a simple example of biotechnology.

fermentation tank

Modern biotechnology

Insulin is a chemical that our bodies naturally produce. It makes sure our bodies take and use sugar from our food. Some people's bodies cannot make insulin. They have a disease called diabetes. Now scientists have taken the **gene** for making insulin from a human. (A gene is a part of a cell that controls how living things grow.) They have then put that gene into bacteria. The bacteria then produce insulin, which can be used by people who are diabetic.

Genetically modified crops

Changing the genetic make-up of a plant can change the way it behaves. Genetically modified (GM) crops look the same as normal crops, but they produce more wheat. Plants have also been changed to make them better at fighting diseases and pests.

IS IT GREEN?

Some people say that GM plants are the answer to food shortages around the world. But others are concerned that we don't know what effect they will have over time. It is good if plants don't need **pesticides** (chemicals that kill the pests that destroy crops). However, if they damage us or the environment, they will do more harm than good.

GM crops cannot be grown in all countries. Some scientists still think the plants might be unsafe.

Bill Clinton launched the Clinton Global Initiative University in 2007. It hosts a yearly meeting for students, national youth organizations, and university officials. They discuss solutions to pressing global issues.

The Presidential Awards

In 1995 the US president, Bill Clinton, launched a series of awards called the Presidential Awards for Green Chemistry Challenge. They have been presented every year since. Many of the awards show how biotechnology can replace traditional chemistry. Advances in biotechnology can mean that chemicals are made in safer, more sustainable ways.

Some winning ideas

• *A medicine to treat diabetes.* This was difficult to make and relied on the use of an expensive, rare metal. A biotechnology company managed to develop a new enzyme that would turn simple chemicals into this medicine.

• *A micro-organism (tiny living thing) that would feed on fats and turn them into biofuels and other chemicals.* A company discovered that, in this way, bacteria can produce many chemicals that would otherwise need complicated, high-energy processes to make them.

Green plants tackle pollution

Explosives are used for military purposes and to demolish old buildings. One commonly used explosive is called RDX. However, when it is used, it causes pollution, leaving behind traces of RDX that are toxic.

Now scientists have found a way to clean up the pollution. They discovered a bacterium that can feed on the RDX. To do so it uses a particular enzyme. The scientists inserted the gene for the enzyme into plants. The plants can then be grown in polluted soil where they will draw out the RDX. The enzyme then breaks it down to nothing.

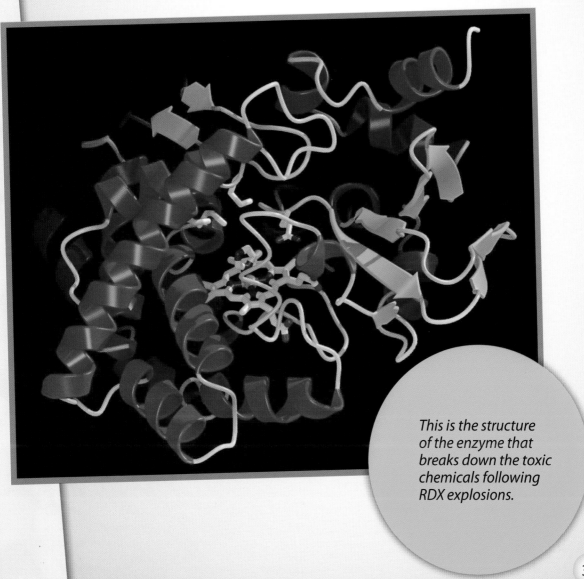

This is the structure of the enzyme that breaks down the toxic chemicals following RDX explosions.

GREEN NANOTECHNOLOGY

A nanometre is one billionth of a metre. **Nanotechnology** uses and makes things in that size range. Scientists have talked about making machines the size of molecules (the smallest part that a substance can be broken down into). Motors and computers would be smaller than a human cell (the smallest building block of living things). <u>Nanotechnology is being used to deliver drugs to diseased cells in the body</u>.

Carbon nanotubes

Carbon **atoms** (tiny pieces of carbon) can be joined together to make a tiny little tube called a nanotube. Long nanotubes can be made into the strongest fibre available. Electricity flows very easily through carbon nanotubes. They could be used to make powerful computers. These uses involve using smaller amounts of material and less energy to achieve better results. This is a good example of what green technology can do.

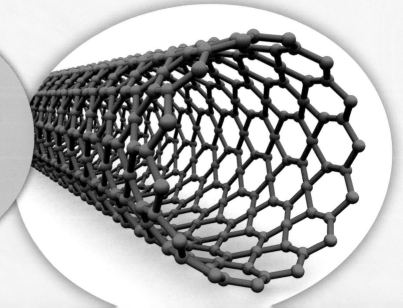

This is a model of a carbon nanotube. Its actual size is 1–2 nanometres in diameter.

This is a computer simulation of platinum nanoparticles (yellow) helping to obtain clean energy from a fuel cell.

NANOTUBES IN CARS

Carbon nanotubes are being used to solve other environmental problems. Researchers in the United States have found that using them as a terminal (central power point) in some types of batteries increases the power of the battery. This could mean that batteries can get smaller or that, when used in a car, a vehicle can travel further.

Water treatment using nanotechnology

There are currently three uses for nanotechnology:

• *Removing pollution from water*. This can often be a challenge. But now nanoparticles are being used to change the dangerous chemicals into harmless ones. This method can be used to reach the pollutants in underground wells. It is much cheaper than pumping the water out for treatment.

• *Turning salty water into drinking water*. This can be done using nano-sized fibres that help remove the salt.

• *Using a filter (strainer) to remove* **viruses** *(germs) from water*. This has so far not been possible. The viruses just go through the filter. Now new materials which have nano-sized holes are being developed that will remove the virus cells.

Green by design

In the future, everything we use will be designed and produced based on whether it is sustainable or not. This will include our buildings, machines, clothes, and chemicals. Architects, clothes designers, engineers, and of course green chemists, are already working in this way. Here are a few examples.

MINI-MACHINES

Do washing machines have to be so huge, take up so much floor space, and use so much water? No, says one designer who has created a small, wall-mounted washing machine.

FAST-GROWING FASHION

One fashion designer based in San Francisco, USA is using fast-growing bamboo and palm-tree straw to make handbags and make-up bags. They also make sunglasses from bamboo.

GREEN GLUE

Millions of carpet tiles are thrown away every year. It is impossible to recycle them because of the glue used to stick them down. Now chemists have designed a starch-based glue that can easily be removed at the end of a carpet's life.

SOLAR SWITCH-OVER

In remote parts of Asia, people living far from mains electricity have to use an oil called kerosene. This is burned in lamps to provide light. Now many people are using solar panels to power lights, mobile phones, and even sewing machines. The cost of the panels is covered by the saving in kerosene costs.

Elithis Tower

Buildings use energy to heat them and for lighting. In offices, energy is needed to operate computers and other machines. The Elithis Tower in Dijon, France is the world's first office block that produces more energy than it uses. It uses solar panels to do this. For this reason, it is called "energy positive".

The future of green technology

Green technology is here to stay. Governments around the world are investing in it. New jobs are being created which use green technology. People know that what they are doing is good for the future of Earth. Many people hope that the term *green technology* will disappear. They hope that everything we make and everything we do will be based on the principles of sustainability. Then no one will need to refer to green technology because all technology will be green.

The Elithis Tower is made of wood and recycled insulation. It has 330 solar panels on its roof.

Glossary

algae tiny green living things that grow in lakes, ponds, and oceans. Many of them can only be seen through a microscope

atom smallest possible piece of a simple substance

bacteria tiny living things

biodegradable breaks down (rots) naturally. Substances that are biodegradable will disappear from the environment in time.

biodiesel vehicle fuel made from plants

biofuel fuel produced from living things. Plants, algae, and bacteria can all produce biofuels.

biotechnology using living things and biological systems to make the materials we want

carbon footprint amount of carbon dioxide produced by the activities of a person or group in a set amount of time

chemicals substances that can be changed into other substances by changing their structure

cylinders in a car engine the fuel (petrol or diesel) is burnt in metal containers called cylinders. The explosion of the burning fuel drives a piston that fits into the cylinder.

eco-house house that has been designed to make it sustainable. It will be energy efficient and will save water.

emission refers to waste substances that are given off from vehicles. In cars, the emissions come out of the exhaust pipe. In aeroplanes, they come straight from the jet engine.

energy fuel for heat, light, and to power vehicles

environment our surroundings. We usually use the word to refer to natural surroundings that can be harmed by human activity.

enzyme complicated chemical in living things that helps to bring about chemical changes. There are many enzymes and each one does a particular job.

fermentation process using yeast that turns sugar into alcohol in the absence of oxygen

fluorescent containing a bright glow. Fluorescent lights contain a gas that glows brightly when electricity is passed through it.

fossil fuel fuel made from dead animals or plants that have been in Earth's crust for millions of years. Coal, oil, and natural gas are the main examples.

gene piece of information that is passed from parents to offspring. Each gene is responsible for one feature of a living thing.

generate create or produce. Used to describe the production of electricity.

greenhouse gas gas that gets into the air and prevents heat leaving Earth. This causes Earth to warm up. Carbon dioxide is the main greenhouse gas.

hybrid combination of two things. For example, a moped is a hybrid because it combines an engine with pedal power.

hydroelectricity production of electricity by water power

insulation material that stops heat passing through it

kerosene fuel commonly used in less developed countries for burning in oil lamps for lighting

nanotechnology science of using or making things that are about the size of atoms

natural resources substances that are found on Earth and can be used by humans

non-renewable will eventually run out before more is made

pesticides chemicals that kill insects that eat crops

photovoltaic using light to produce electricity

pollution contamination of the environment by harmful substances such as chemicals

power station factory where electricity is produced

recycle take an object or material that has been used for one purpose and re-process it so that it can be used again

renewable energy energy sources that will not run out. Solar, wind, waves, and tides are examples.

rotor moving part of a motor which spins around

sensor device that will detect changes in the surroundings. It might detect heat, light, or movement.

silicon chemical that is a partial conductor of electricity and as a result is used in computer parts

solar related to the Sun. Solar energy comes from the Sun.

sustainable able to keep going. A sustainable lifestyle is one that only uses things that we can keep getting more of.

toxic poisonous

turbine machine that has blades that can be turned by wind, water, or steam. The blades drive a shaft that then turns a generator to make electricity.

virus tiny infectious thing that reproduces in the cells of a plant or animal

Find out more

Books

Mates, Dates and Saving the Planet, Cathy Hopkins (Piccadilly Press, 2008)

Superkids! 250 Incredible Ways to Save the Planet, Sasha Norris (Think Publishing, 2005)

Why Should I Bother About the Planet? Jane Chisholm (Usborne Publishing, 2010)

The Usborne Science Encyclopedia (Usborne Publishing, 2010)

Websites

How Stuff Works
www.howstuffworks.com
Search here to find out how car engines, electric and hybrid cars, turbines, solar power, and many other things work.

Alternative energy sources
www.neok12.com/Energy-Sources.htm
Find out more about all the green energy sources covered in this book. There are videos, games, and quizzes.

Explain that stuff
www.explainthatstuff.com/nanotechnologyforkids.html
This link gives a clear explanation of nanotechnology, with some examples.

David Suzuki Foundation
www.davidsuzuki.org/what-you-can-do
This site gives you ideas on how to create healthy and sustainable homes and communities.

Eco Kids
www.ecokids.ca/pub/index.cfm
This is an environmental education site for kids and teachers with games and activities.

Topics to research

Green companies

Find out about factories or businesses that use green ideas. There may be green companies in your area. Do you think people feel better about the way these companies work?

Solar power

Find out more about Solar Impulse. What other kinds of vehicles can be powered by the Sun?

Green points

From 2011, the UK government is offering a £5,000 grant to people who buy certain electric cars. There are also plans to install thousands of power points for recharging electric car batteries in different regions of the country. Find out where these regions are. Think about whether this will help make electric cars more popular.

Index